DOGS SET III

Jack Russell Terriers

Bob Temple

ABDO Publishing Company

visit us at
www.abdopub.com

Published by ABDO Publishing Company, 4940 Viking Drive, Suite 622, Edina, Minnesota 55435.

Printed in the United States.

Edited by: Paul Joseph

Photo credits: Peter Arnold, Inc.; Ron Kimball Photography

Library of Congress Cataloging-in-Publication Data

Temple, Bob.
      Jack Russell terriers / Bob Temple
              p. cm. — (Dogs. Set III)
      ISBN 1-57765-424-2
      1. Jack Russell terrier—Juvenile literature. [1. Jack Russell terrier. 2. Dogs. 3. Pets] I. Title.

SF429.J27 T46 2000
636.755—dc21
                            00-038049

Contents

Where Dogs Come From

Dogs and humans have been together for thousands of years. Originally, most dogs were wild and hunted in packs. There are still some types of wild dogs, such as wolves and foxes. These wild dogs are part of the same family of animals as the dogs we keep as family pets. All dogs come from the species called Canidae, from the Latin word canis, which means "dog."

Many types of dogs are just happy to be family pets. They like to play with children, go on walks, or sleep in the house. Other types of dogs like to work, too. Some dogs help farmers herd sheep. Others help on hunting trips with their owners. The Jack Russell Terrier is one such dog.

Opposite page: The Jack Russell Terrier, like all dogs, is related to the wolf.

Jack Russell Terriers

The Jack Russell Terrier is from the "terrier" group of dogs. These dogs are usually very smart, tough dogs. They also have lots of energy. The Jack Russell Terrier has so much energy, it seems like it is always on the move.

The Jack Russell Terrier was developed in the 19th century in England. A clergyman named Jack Russell started the **breed**. This very small but feisty dog was used to hunt small animals, such as foxes. To do this, the dog would dig into the animal's underground home to force the animals out. Some Jack Russell Terriers are still used in this manner today.

The Jack Russell Terrier got its name from the man who started the breed, Jack Russell.

What They're Like

Jack Russell Terriers are very active dogs. They are not very big, but are very perky and have a strong spirit. Most Jack Russells are not afraid of anything. They are very smart and will obey their owner if they are trained properly. They are good with children who do not tease or hit them. If they are well-trained, they can be good family pets. They sometimes are not very good with other dogs, because they like to fight.

Many Jack Russell Terriers live indoors with their human families. But they need lots of exercise and plenty of time outside. They are best off in a house with at least a small yard in which they can play. Because they have been bred to hunt small animals, they are not good with other family pets like rabbits or guinea pigs. They have to be kept away from these animals, or the dog might hurt them.

Jack Russells are very active and agile dogs. They can also jump very high.

Coat and Color

A Jack Russell Terrier's **coat** can either be smooth or "broken." A smooth coat has thick hairs that are flat against the dog's body. There is usually a lot of hair. A broken coat has a short, thick undercoat covered by a straight, longer coat. Jack Russell Terriers don't usually have curly or wavy hair.

They are mostly white, with black or tan markings on their bodies. Most often, the markings are on the dog's head and ears, and near his tail. Their body stays mostly white. Many Jack Russell Terriers have a white face with brown or black spot that covers their ears and the area around their eyes.

Opposite page: Jack Russells tend to have markings on their face and ears.

Size

Jack Russell Terriers are small dogs. They stand between 12 and 14 inches (30 and 36 cm) at the shoulders. They usually weigh between 13 and 17 pounds (5.9 and 7.7 kg).

Their heads are long and thin, not round. Their ears are v-shaped and hang down in front. Their noses are black and their almond-shaped eyes are dark. The short tail stands straight up.

Opposite page: Jack Russell Terriers are small dogs but also very strong.

Care

Jack Russell Terriers need lots of love and attention. Mostly, they need lots of exercise. A Jack Russell Terrier that gets the right amount of exercise will be less likely to go off on his own and get into trouble. If he has a small yard to play in, he will be able to exercise himself. However, sometimes they like to dig holes and try to hunt.

When you take your Jack Russell Terrier for a walk, you shouldn't let him off his leash. He might try to go off hunting for small animals!

The Jack Russell Terrier's **coat** is easy to manage. Combing and brushing it regularly will help keep it healthy. They don't need to be bathed very often, either.

Like all dogs, Jack Russell Terriers need to see the **veterinarian** at least once a year. At the veterinarian, they will get the tests and the shots they need to stay healthy. These shots protect the dog against diseases like **distemper** and **rabies**.

Jack Russells are very active and love to be taken on long walks.

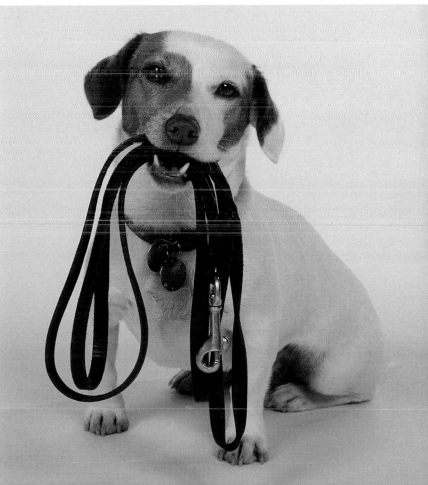

Feeding

Good **nutrition** is important for every dog. Without the right food, your Jack Russell Terrier won't be a happy, healthy member of the family.

When you are just starting out with a puppy, you should ask the breeder what type of food the dog was getting. Then, you should continue to use that food for your dog. Changing a dog's food has to be done slowly. Otherwise, the dog will get an upset stomach and can become sick.

Puppies usually eat several small meals each day. As they get older, fewer feedings are needed. Most adult dogs only eat once each day. If your Jack Russell Terrier is getting a well-balanced **diet**, he will be happy and healthy. Dogs need different types of food at different times in their lives. Young

dogs need food that will give them lots of energy. Your dog's **veterinarian** can help you decide what is the best food for your dog. And you should always make sure to have plenty of clean, fresh water for your dog to drink.

By the time your Jack Russell is full grown it will only need one feeding per day.

Things They Need

Since the Jack Russell Terrier loves to play so much, you should make sure he has plenty of toys to keep him busy. Balls, tug-of-war ropes, and bones will help keep him happy. He also needs a quiet place to rest when he gets tired. A dog bed or blanket in a quiet spot in the house will help.

Jack Russell Terriers can live in an apartment if you make sure to take them outside every day to get the exercise they need. It is best if you live near a park or a place where they can run on their leash. A small yard is better. A Jack Russell Terrier will be happiest in a place where they have plenty of room to run and play. They will be even happier if they get a chance to hunt a little.

Opposite page: Jack Russells love to play and be active.

Like all dogs, your Jack Russell Terrier needs a collar with a tag that includes your name, address, and telephone number. That way if the dog gets lost, you can be called by the person who finds it. In most cities, dogs also need a **license**. Most dogs also wear a tag that says they have gotten their **rabies** shot.

Most importantly, your dog needs to be trained correctly. A well-trained dog will be a better member of the family. That way, both you and your dog are happier.

Puppies

Jack Russell Terriers can have five puppies in a **litter**. When a Jack Russell Terrier is **pregnant**, it will try to make a place to have its puppies. You should give her a strong box in a dark, warm place in your house. Put a blanket in the box. She will have her puppies there. Most important, if you find out your Jack Russell Terrier is pregnant, get lots of help from your **veterinarian**.

Puppies are very helpless when they are born. All dogs are **mammals**, which means they drink milk from their mother's body when they are newborns. After about four weeks, you can begin to feed them soft puppy food. At this time, they need less and less of their mother's milk. This is called weaning.

Jack Russell Terriers need to get used to people and other dogs when they are young. That way, they will behave better when they are older. As long as you treat them kindly when they are puppies, they will grow up to love humans as much as we love them.

The Jack Russell Terrier is very small when it is a puppy.

Glossary

breed: a group of dogs that share the same appearance and characteristics.

coat: the hair that covers a dog's body.

diet: the food that your dog eats.

distemper: a contagious disease that dogs sometimes get. It is caused by a virus.

license (LIE-sense): a tag worn by a dog indicating it has been registered with a city.

litter: the group of puppies a dog has in one pregnancy.

mammal: warm-blooded animals that feed their babies milk from the mother's body.

nutrition (new-TRISH-un): food; nourishment.

pregnant: with one or more babies growing within the body.

rabies: a dangerous disease that dogs can get.

veterinarian (VET-er-in-AIR-ian): your dog's doctor; also called a vet.

Internet Sites

Jack Russell Terrier Club of America
www.terrier.com

This site is full of helpful advice for the person who is interested in owning a Jack Russell Terrier. Learn about the breed and its history. Read about upcoming events and dog shows. You can even join the club if you want. There is also a place where you can post a question about Jack Russell Terriers.

Jack Russell Terrier Association of America
www. jrtaa.org

At this site, you can find out about the history of the breed and of the club. You can also learn about breeders, rescue organizations, and even find a list of books that are about Jack Russell Terriers. There is a page of photos of the dogs, too.

Index